Space Explorer

WORKING IN SPACE

Patricia Whitehouse

www.heinemann.co.uk/library
Visit our website to find out more information about *Heinemann Library* books.

To order:

 Phone 44 (0)1865 888066

 Send a fax to 44 (0)1865 314091

Visit the Heinemann Bookshop at **www.heinemann.co.uk/library** to browse our catalogue and order online.

First published in Great Britain by Heinemann Library, Halley Court, Jordan Hill, Oxford OX2 8EJ, part of Harcourt Education. Heinemann is a registered trademark of Harcourt Education Ltd.

Editorial: Jilly Attwood and Kate Bellamy
Design: Ron Kamen and Paul Davies
Picture Research: Ruth Blair and Sally Claxton
Production: Séverine Ribierre

Originated by Dot Gradations Ltd
Printed and bound in China by South China Printing Company

The paper used to print this book comes from sustainable resources.

ISBN 0 431 11346 7
08 07 06 05 04
10 9 8 7 6 5 4 3 2 1

British Library Cataloguing in Publication Data

Whitehouse, Patty
Working in Space – (Space Explorer)
629.4'5

A full catalogue record for this book is available from the British Library.

Acknowledgements

The Publishers are grateful to the following for permission to reproduce photographs: Getty Images p. **27** (Photodisc); NASA pp. **4**, **5**, **6**, **8**, **9**, **10**, **11**, **12**, **15**, **17**, **18**, **19**, **21**, **22**, **24**, **26**, **28**; Science Photo Library pp. **7**, **13**, **14**, **16**, **23**, **25**, **29** (NASA); Topham p. **20** (Photri)

Cover photo reproduced with permission of NASA.

Our thanks to Stuart Clark for his assistance in the preparation of this book.

Every effort has been made to contact copyright holders of any material reproduced in this book. Any omissions will be rectified in subsequent printings if notice is given to the Publishers.

Contents

Words written in bold, **like this,** are explained in the Glossary.

 Find out more about space at www.heinemannexplore.co.uk.

Leaving Earth

5...4...3...2...1... The space
shuttle blasts off! **Astronauts**
on the shuttle are going to work.
Some stay on the shuttle and
some work at the **space station**.

Two astronauts have already started working. The Shuttle Commander is in charge of the shuttle and crew. The Pilot flies the shuttle.

Three Mission Specialists are on board the shuttle. They work on **experiments**, or climb outside to fix **satellites**. They have to prepare the food, too.

6

This Mission Specialist is measuring how far away the Hubble Space Telescope is from their space shuttle.

A company or university might do an experiment in space. They choose a **Payload Specialist** who goes to space to work on their experiment.

The Payload Specialist may have trained for two years just for this mission.

Working in space

Earth's **gravity** pulls everything towards the Earth's centre. In space the Earth's pull is not very strong. **Astronauts** live in **microgravity**. This means they float around.

8

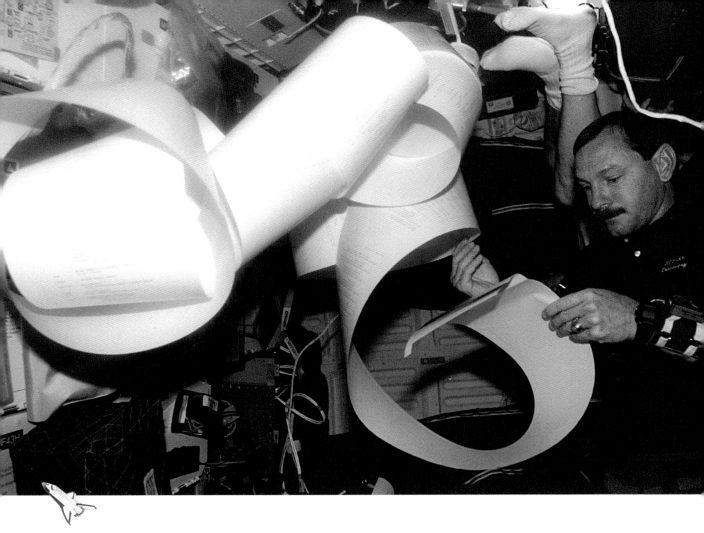

A long sheet of fax paper floats
in low gravity.

Astronauts do not work at desks and
tables. Everything would float off because
there is not much gravity! They have to
use tape to stick everything down.

Astronauts need special training. They study at university and then do a year of basic astronaut training. Astronauts learn maths, science, and **astronomy**. They also practise using space equipment.

Some equipment shows astronauts what it will be like to work in the International **Space Station**

10

Astronauts practise working in water. Their suits are filled with air to make them float. It helps them learn what it will be like in space.

Under water it feels like you weigh less than on land. This is what it is like in space.

Experiments on astronauts

Living in space can change the human body. **Astronauts** are often part of **experiments** to find out how to keep healthy in space.

This experiment measures how much air the astronaut uses when she exercises.

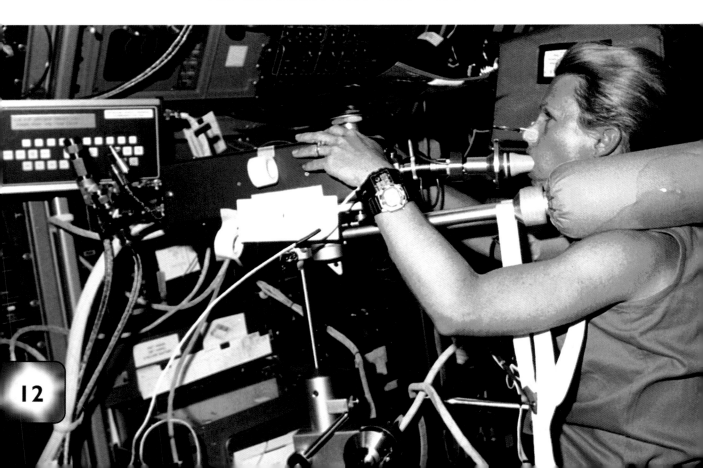

In space, astronauts do not use their bones and muscles very much. They can get very weak. Astronauts need to exercise every day in space.

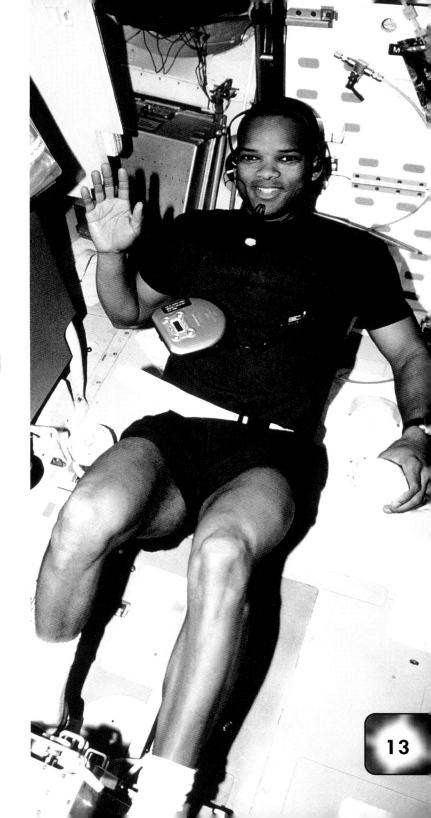

Other experiments

Scientists want to find out how living in space affects plants and animals. **Astronauts** have taken bees, ants and fish into space to see what happens to them.

This **experiment** looked at how bean plants grow in space.

Astronauts also test to see what happens to chemicals in space. They use a sealed box with gloves sticking into it so the experiment does not float away.

Astronauts put their hands in the gloves so they can move objects around in the box.

Astronauts also take pictures and videos of themselves living in space. The photos help people on Earth understand what it is like to live in space.

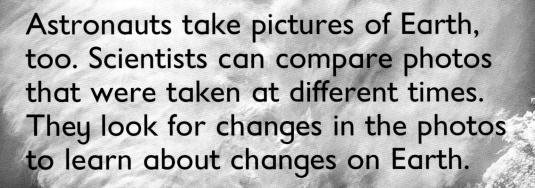

Astronauts take pictures of Earth, too. Scientists can compare photos that were taken at different times. They look for changes in the photos to learn about changes on Earth.

Astronauts in space took this picture of a volcano erupting.

Fixing satellites

Satellites that **orbit** the Earth sometimes break down and need repairing. They cannot be taken to a workshop. Specially trained **astronauts** have to fix them.

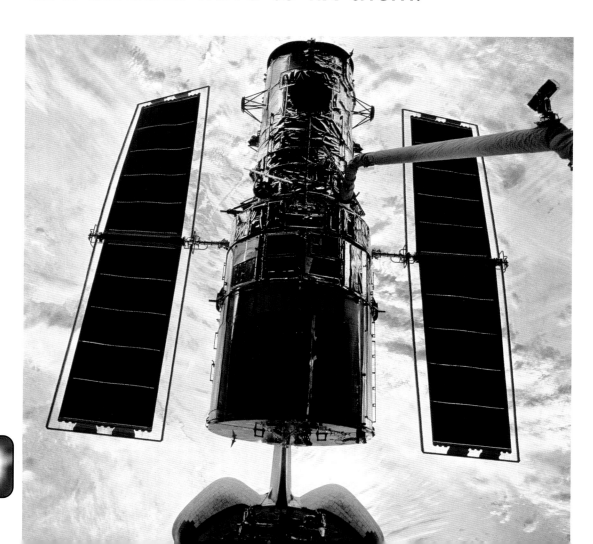

The Shuttle Pilot finds the satellite and moves the shuttle near to it. An astronaut uses the shuttle's **robotic arm** to pull the satellite into the shuttle's cargo bay.

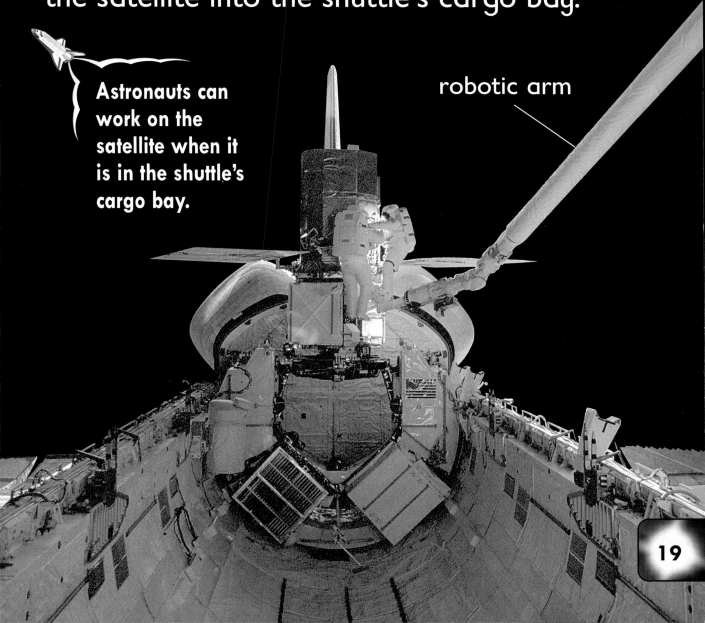

Astronauts can work on the satellite when it is in the shuttle's cargo bay.

robotic arm

People who work outside on Earth sometimes wear special clothing. Some clothing protects workers. Some clothing makes them stand out so they can be seen easily.

These clothes are worn to protect the worker.

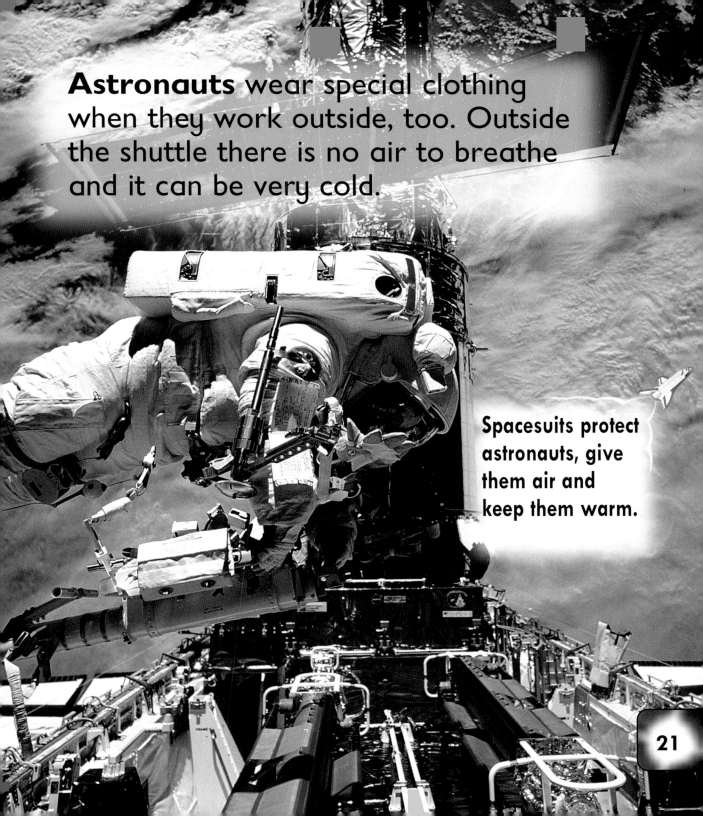

Astronauts wear special clothing when they work outside, too. Outside the shuttle there is no air to breathe and it can be very cold.

Spacesuits protect astronauts, give them air and keep them warm.

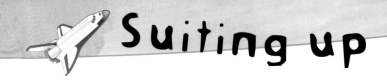

Suiting up

Astronauts must wear special spacesuits to go out of the shuttle. The spacesuits allow the astronauts to breathe and stay warm. Every part of their bodies is covered.

Spacesuits are sealed at the neck, wrists and waist.

Astronauts use an **airlock** to leave the shuttle. The airlock is a room between the shuttle and space. In the airlock, the door to the shuttle seals shut and then the outer door into space can be opened.

Using an airlock stops air from the shuttle leaking into space.

Gloves and ties

Spacesuits are hard to move in.
Gloves make finger movements tricky.
Jobs that take a few minutes on Earth
can take hours in space.

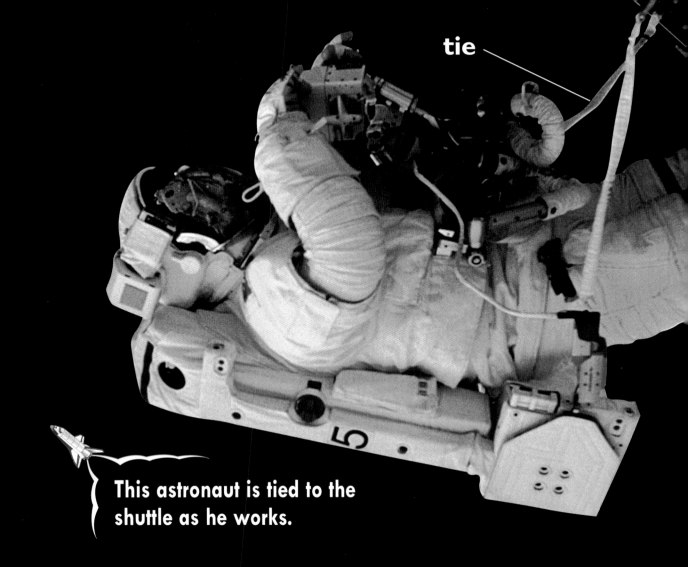

tie

This astronaut is tied to the
shuttle as he works.

In space, **astronauts** and equipment
can float away. Astronauts tie
equipment to their suits. Sometimes
astronauts are tied to the shuttle, too.

Sometimes **astronauts** need to move around a lot outside the shuttle. They wear a backpack with rocket power called a **Manned Manoeuvring Unit**, or **MMU**.

The MMU tank is filled with gas. The astronaut squeezes a handle and gas comes out with enough force to move the astronaut around.

Working on other worlds

Twelve **astronauts** have worked on the Moon. They collected rocks from the Moon's surface. This helped scientists learn about Earth, and about living on other worlds.

Scientists controlled where Sojourner went on Mars and Sojourner sent photos back to Earth.

Scientists explored Mars using a remote-controlled robot called Sojourner. Scientists think that in the future people might be able to live and work on Mars.

Amazing space facts

- The longest time an **astronaut** has spent outside in a spacesuit is 8 hours and 56 minutes.

- It takes about 45 minutes for an astronaut to put on a spacesuit. Astronauts must help each other to put a spacesuit on.

- The largest-sized spacesuit weighs 48.6 kilograms. That is the same as 105 bags of sugar.

- In the USA, over 4000 people apply for 10 astronaut jobs each year.

 Find out more about space at www.heinemannexplore.co.uk.

Glossary

airlock space between two doors that keeps air from escaping

astronauts people who go into space

experiments tests

gravity a force that pulls objects together

Manned Manoeuvring Unit (MMU) a backpack with rocket power

microgravity gravity that is very, very weak

orbit the path one object takes around another

Payload Specialist astronaut working on university or company experiments

robotic arm remote controlled machine that can grab or move things

satellite an object that orbits a planet or a moon

space station a place where astronauts work and live in space

More books and websites

Space Explorer Atlas, Richard Platt and Leo Hartas
(Dorling Kindersley Publishing, 1999)
Living in Space (Space Explorer), Patricia Whitehouse
(Heinemann Library, 2004)
Space Travel (Space Explorer), Patricia Whitehouse (Heinemann Library, 2004)

www.esa.int
www.nasa.gov/audiencce/forkids

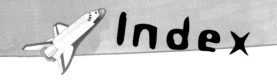

Index

Titles in the *Space Explorer* series include:

Hardback   0 431 11347 5

Hardback   0 431 11348 3

Hardback   0 431 11345 9

Hardback   0 431 11342 4

Hardback   0 431 11341 6

Hardback   0 431 11344 0

Hardback   0 431 11343 2

Hardback   0 431 11340 8

Hardback   0 431 11346 7

Find out about the other titles in this series on our website www.heinemann.co.uk/library